LITTLE TIGER

LONDON

CATERPILLAR BOOKS
An imprint of the Little Tiger Group
www.littletiger.co.uk
1 Coda Studios, 189 Munster Road, London SW6 6AW
First published in Great Britain 2020
Text by Isabel Otter • Text copyright © Caterpillar Books Ltd 2020
Illustrations copyright © Fernando Martin 2020
A CIP catalogue record for this book is available from the British Library
ISBN: 978-1-83891-033-4
CPB/1400/1411/0620
2 4 6 8 10 9 7 5 3 1

I am a BiRD

Welcome!

I will take you on a tour
of the skies and introduce you
to some of my feathered friends!

My hard, pointy **beak** is perfect for pecking! Some birds have tough beaks that can crack nuts. Others have small, delicate beaks for picking up insects.

beak

Birds don't have teeth. We swallow our food whole! Sometimes we eat grit to help grind it down.

Look at my wings! They allow me to **fly.** When I flap them up and down I can lift myself into the air.

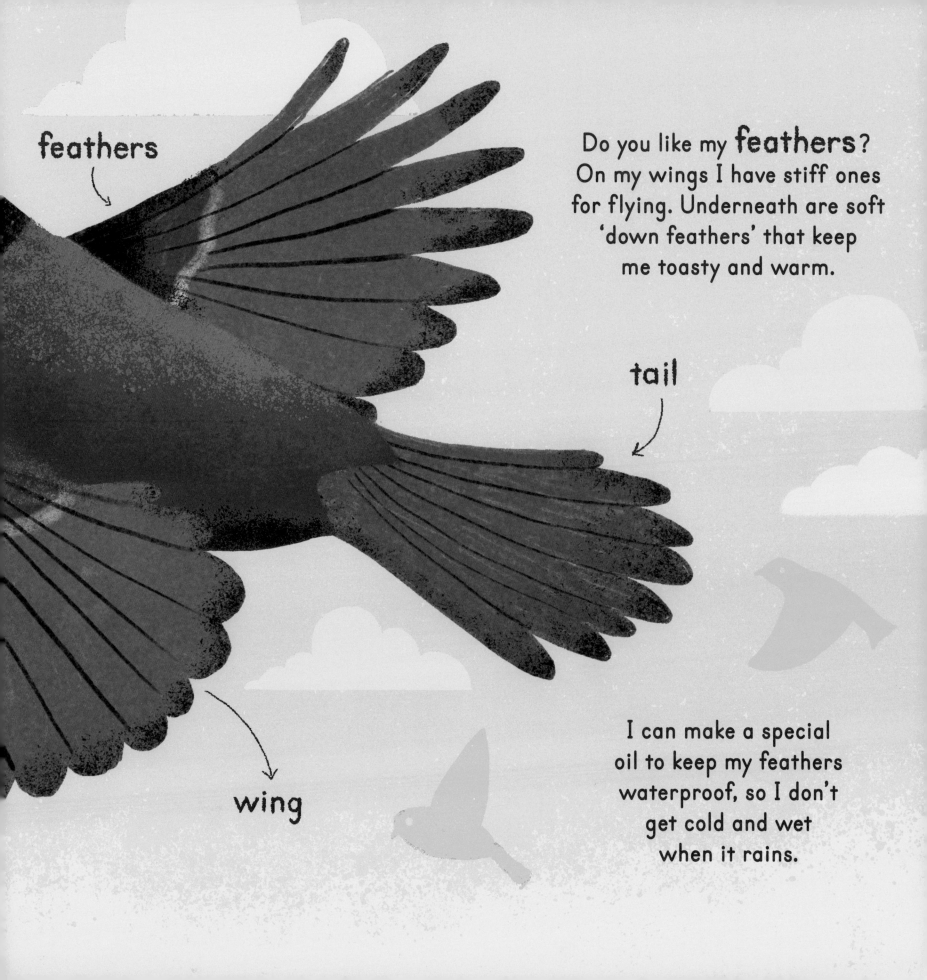

feathers

Do you like my **feathers**? On my wings I have stiff ones for flying. Underneath are soft 'down feathers' that keep me toasty and warm.

tail

wing

I can make a special oil to keep my feathers waterproof, so I don't get cold and wet when it rains.

Not all birds build nests. Woodpeckers make holes in trees to lay their eggs in.

Nests come in all shapes and sizes.

They are a place to lay eggs and keep baby birds safe.

Hanging nests are **woven** using grass and leaves. Weaver birds can tie knots with their beaks!

Puffins like
to lay their eggs
in underground
burrows.

Some water birds build nests that float on lakes or rivers.
Often they use plants as anchors to stop
their nests from floating away.

Baby birds hatch out of eggs.

The mother sits on the eggs to keep them warm, dry and safe.

Cheep!

When they are ready
to **hatch**, the baby birds
break out of their shells
with their newly
grown beaks.

Then they
grow into little
chicks!

The cuckoo lays
its eggs in other birds'
nests, tricking them into
looking after its brood!

Ostrich eggs are
the largest in the
world. Each one can
be as big as a melon.

Why do birds sing?

Calls are used as warnings or to say hello. Baby birds call out when they are hungry.

Birds sing to attract mates and warn other birds off their territories.

Some birds dance in order to impress future partners!

Songs are longer and more complicated than calls. Some birds know thousands of different songs!

What do birds eat?

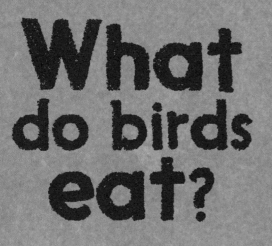

Birds eat all sorts of things, depending on where they live and how they behave.

Seagulls do a 'rain dance' to catch worms.

They stamp on the ground, tricking worms into thinking that it is raining...

When the worms come above ground, the gulls gobble them up!

Vultures and condors
eat the leftovers of
other animals.

Eagles can swoop to catch fish.

Some birds,
like this cardinal,
are happiest scoffing
seeds and berries.

Why do birds migrate?

When the weather gets colder, certain birds travel from one place to another to find food and to breed.

The Arctic tern has the longest migration of any bird. It flies across the world, from the Arctic to Antarctica and back again six months later.

Geese fly in a special V-shape when they migrate, taking it in turns to lead the group.

Travelling birds find their way using the Sun, Moon, stars and landmarks.

Birds come from all over the world.

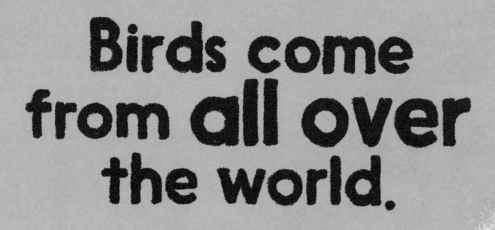

Golden eagles live in the mountains and hunt small animals.

There aren't many trees in mountain regions, which makes it easier for the eagles to spot prey from the air.

Eagle wings are among the most powerful in the animal kingdom.

Woodland
is a popular habitat.
Trees offer birds food,
shelter and safety.

Birds that live in the hot,
dry **desert** need to survive
with very little water.

The cactus wren
makes its nest inside
these spiky plants.

Not all birds can fly!

Here are some examples...

Kiwis sleep in burrows during the day and forage for food at night. Their feathers are soft and feel like hair.

Kakapos are a type of owl parrot. They are one of the rarest birds in the world.

Most penguins live in Antarctica. On land they
have to walk at a slow waddle but in the sea
they swim with amazing grace and speed.

Penguins stop their eggs from
freezing by warming them in
a special feathered pouch
just above their feet.

Some birds live near water.

Most water birds have **webbed feet,** which help them to swim faster.

Some birds have incredibly long legs that they use to wade into rivers and lakes in search of food.

Gannets have an unusual tactic for catching fish – they dive-bomb into the sea at high speed. Their streamlined shape is perfect for gliding through water.

Snowy owls live in
Arctic regions.

They can hear prey hiding beneath
layers of snow. Their wings are so
powerful that they can knock
over a human being.

Only the hardiest
of birds can survive in
the harsh Arctic climate.
The average temperature
is -40°C (-40°F)!

Snow petrels
nest in the rock
to stay out of the
chilly wind.

Meet the **biggest** bird in the world.

It's an **ostrich!**
This bird comes from
Africa and is very tall.

Its long neck helps
it to keep a look-out
for predators.

If an ostrich feels threatened,
it will lie down flat on the ground
with its neck stretched out
in order to hide.

Ostriches are very fast runners and can sprint at double the speed of humans!

Meet the
smallest **bird**
in the world.

It is the bee hummingbird.

This tiny bird is not
much bigger than the
eye of an ostrich!

Its long, thin
beak is perfect for
sipping nectar
from flowers.

Hummingbirds can beat
their wings up to 80 times
a second! This allows them
to hover in mid-air while
drinking nectar.

We are all birds!

Goodbye!
We hope you enjoyed
your tour of the skies.
Which was your
favourite bird?

*No worms were
harmed in the making
of this book!*